Contents

running

The children are **running**.

Running is a way to move around.

scooter

This is a **scooter**.

The boy zooms down the hill.

bicycle

This is a **bicycle**.

The bicycle moves fast!

bus

This is a **bus**.

The children are waiting
for the **bus**.

truck

This is a **truck**.

The **truck** moves some heavy wood.

helicopter

This is a helicopter.

This helicopter is landing on a beach.

tractor

This is a **tractor**.

The **tractor** moves slowly down the field.

motorbike

These are **motorbikes**.

The **motorbikes** are in a race.

plane

This is a plane.

The plane flies high in the sky.

train

This is a **train**.

A **train** moves along tracks.

traffic

This is a **traffic** jam.

The cars and lorries cannot move!

Picture quiz

Can you find these things in the book?

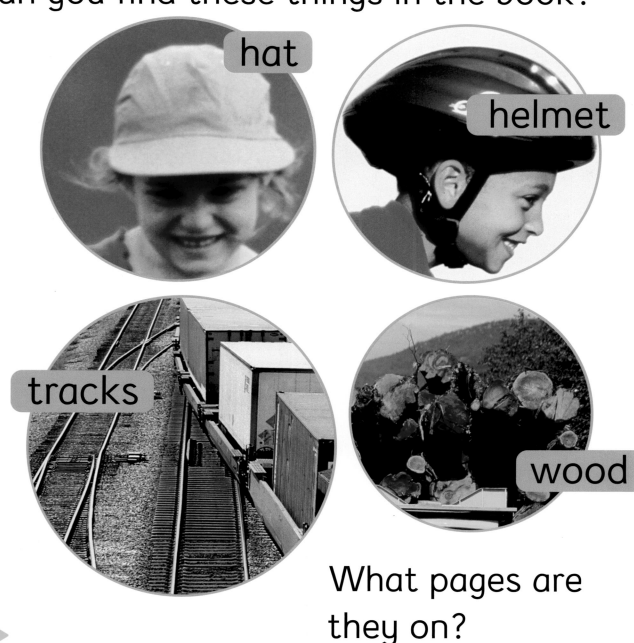

hat

helmet

tracks

wood

What pages are they on?

Index quiz

The index is on page 24.
Use the index and pictures
to answer these questions.

1. Which page shows a truck?
   What colour is the truck?

2. Which pages show children running?
   How many children are there?

3. Which page shows motorbikes?
   What number is on the first motorbike?

4. Which page shows a tractor?
   What colour is the field?

Index

Answers

Picture quiz: The hat is on page 4, the helmet is on page 6, the tracks are on page 19, the wood is on page 10.
Index quiz: 1. page 10, yellow; 2. pages 4-5, five; 3. page 16, number 3; 4. page 15, green and brown.